CONTENTS

Y0-DOJ-719

Robert Vermes, from Topolcany in Slovakia, was born in 1924. Arrested on 27 March 1942, he was deported to the Majdanek concentration camp, where he was murdered.

Malka Malach witnessed the 1939 German invasion of Dąbrowa Gornicza, Poland. She did not survive war and persecution. The exact circumstances of her death are unknown.

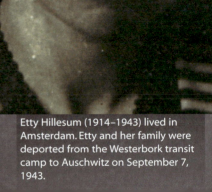

Etty Hillesum (1914–1943) lived in Amsterdam. Etty and her family were deported from the Westerbork transit camp to Auschwitz on September 7, 1943.

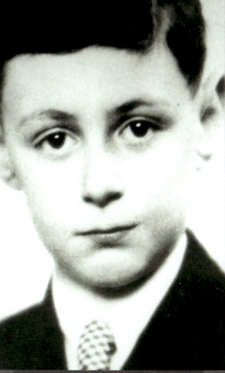

Zdenek Konas, from Prague, was deported to Theresienstadt on July 8, 1943, aged eleven, and sent from there to Auschwitz on September 6, 1943. There has been no trace of him since.

Shimon Mendel from Romania was deported to Auschwitz in 1944 at the age of 59 and murdered there.

Claire Brodzki from Lyon, France, survived deportation to Auschwitz, but died a few months after the liberation of the camp, on June 20, 1945.

THE MEMORIAL IN BERLIN

"We came across the memorial completely by chance, we didn't even know what it was."

Half-way between the bustle of Potsdamer Platz and the austerity of Pariser Platz – home to the Brandenburg Gate and financial and cultural buildings in classicistic style – one's attention is drawn to a vast site the size of two football fields. The site is located opposite the Tiergarten, the largest park in Berlin, and in the direct vicinity of the Federal Chancellery and the Reichstag, the political heart of unified Germany. It houses the Memorial to the Murdered Jews of Europe, which consists of 2,711 blank concrete stelae and an underground Information Centre. The impetus for the Memorial came from a citizens' initiative. In 1999 the German Bundestag passed a resolution to establish the Memorial, which is funded by the German state

"It makes a real impact; it's a bit like a labyrinth or a maze. But what has it got to do with the Holocaust?"

The grey rectangular blocks, arranged in a grid pattern, are known as stelae, from the Greek word for gravestone. No two stelae are alike; they vary in height and are set at different angles. Depending on the season, time of day and light conditions the sun casts a silver, blueish or pale orange sheen onto the stone surfaces. In rain or fog the water rolling off the sides of the stelae leaves unusual patterns and snow creates strange frozen pillows that tilt against each other on top of the stelae.

"Are they meant to represent gravestones? Or a deserted town? Or perhaps even a long row of freight wagons used for deportations?"

The gap between the stelae is too narrow for two people to walk side by side; a person need only take one turning to be lost from view. It is noticeably colder in the centre of the Field of Stelae than on the edges or outside the memorial. The surrounding city retreats and other people can only be seen or heard where the passageways cross. Visitors are occasionally startled when they suddenly encounter other people within the Field of Stelae.

"You feel really uncertain and alone in there, everything is muffled and distant. I found it quite creepy."

People taking part in guided tours engage in heated discussions. Visitors with cameras stand on some of the blocks. Children play tig in the passageways. Tourists sit on the low blocks at the edge of the memorial, relaxing or leafing through travel guides.

"It's just not right, why doesn't anyone say anything to them? It is a memorial after all!"

Coaches drive past or park alongside the memorial. There is a row of souvenir shops and snackbars in the background. People are queuing by some steps right on the edge of the Field of Stelae. They are speaking a variety of languages; one can make out German, English, Polish, Spanish and Dutch. A member of staff hands out a leaflet on the Memorial to the

Murdered Jews of Europe and invites them to visit the exhibition in the Information Centre – entrance is free. There is a security check downstairs. On entering the exhibition, one reads a quotation from the Holocaust survivor Primo Levi: "It happened, therefore it can happen again: this is the core of what we have to say". There are also six large portraits. These show Malka Malach from Poland, Etty Hillesum from the Netherlands, Claire Brodzki from France, Schimon Medel from Romania, Robert Vermes from Slovakia and Zdenek Konas from what is now the Czech Republic. Suddenly the Holocaust has faces, names and life stories. The Field of Stelae then reappears in the individual rooms – as a panelled ceiling or illuminated glass panels. Having visited the exhibition, one leaves "the Ort", as even the American architect Peter Eisenman calls his construction, by going up a flight of steps which leads back into the Field of Stelae. It is at this point, if not before, that the initial sense of alienation occasioned by the unusual architecture disappears. Something has changed.

THE LOCATION OF THE MEMORIAL: HISTORY AND DEBATE

Since May 2005, the Field of Stelae with its 2,711 concrete blocks has become such an integral part of the German capital that it seems as if it has always been there. The years of debate in the 1990s over whether to build such a national memorial, the form it should take and to whom it should be dedicated are almost forgotten.

The memorial was originally proposed in 1988 by a citizens' initiative led by the historian Eberhard Jäckel and the publicist Lea Rosh. In the years that followed, the Association Memorial to the Murdered Jews of Europe won broad public support for the project. The initial plan was to build the memorial on the site of the former SS Reich Main Security Office in Prinz-Albrecht-Strasse (now Niederkirchnerstrasse). It was only after the fall of the Berlin Wall and the dismantling of the GDR border strip in 1989–90 that the idea arose to construct the memorial on the barren land between Behren-strasse and Voßstrasse, near the former Reich Chancellery of Adolf Hitler and the "Führerbunker". The Federal Ministry of the Interior, the Berlin Senate's Department of Culture and the Association Memorial to the Murdered Jews of Europe agreed on this site in spring 1992.

The memorial is located on a site measuring around 19,000 m² on the edge of the Tiergarten Park that was part of the "Ministry Gardens" (Ministergärten) until 1945. This area was developed after 1688 and became the third enlargement of medieval Berlin during the Baroque period. At the heart of the development was the Wilhelmstrasse, the construction of which commenced in 1732. Seven palaces or palatial buildings were built in this section of the Wilhelmstrasse, each with an ornamental garden. In the course of the 19th century, state institutions and ministries from Prussia and later the German Reich moved into this area. The Wilhelmstrasse was

to become a centre of Prussian-German administration and the grounds located to the rear of the buildings became the Ministry Gardens. The memorial is built on a plot that once housed the gardens of Wilhelmstrasse 72 and 73.

The buildings and grounds of Wilhelmstrasse 72, which were redesigned on a number of occasions, initially belonged to the court president Hans Christoph von Görne. At the beginning of the 19th century they became the property of the Prussian King, until the state acquired them from the Hohenzollern dynasty in 1919. The following year, the newly established Reich Ministry for Nutrition (later the Reich Ministry for Nutrition and Agriculture) moved into the building, where it remained until the building was destroyed in February 1945. In 1937, Reich Propaganda Minister Joseph Goebbels had a villa constructed on the site to house his offices. A bunker was added three years later. The rubble from the destroyed building was cleared after 1945, but the bunker remained intact.

Wilhelmstrasse 73 was constructed as the palace of Count von Sacken. In the mid-19th century, this building and its gardens were purchased by the King and served as the ministry for the Royal Family until the dissolution of the monarchy. The property was acquired by the state in 1919 and became the offices and residence of the newly-established post of Reich President. Paul von Hindenburg was thus to live here from 1925 to 1934. From 1938, the palace was used by the Reich Foreign Minister Joachim von Ribbentrop, before it was burnt down as the result of bombing raids in spring 1945.

The ruins of both buildings were cleared in the early 1960s. With the construction of the Berlin Wall by the GDR in 1961, the gardens disappeared and became part of the "death strip". After the border fortifications were dismantled in 1989–90, the site of the former Ministry Gardens remained a wasteland until it was selected as the location for the national Holocaust memorial.

In the mid-1990s, there were two architectural competitions to decide on the form that the memorial would take. On June 25, 1999 the Bundestag held a vote on the memorial in one of its final sessions in the former West German

Soviet "T 34" tanks in front of the wall surrounding the Ministry Gardens, Ebertstrasse, May 1945.

Initial border fortifications in East Berlin as preparation for the construction of the Berlin Wall, Ebertstrasse, August 13, 1961, 12 p.m.

honour the six million Jews murdered by the National Socialists; to keep alive the memory of these inconceivable events in German history; and to admonish future generations to never again violate human rights, to defend the democratic constitutional state at all times, to secure equality before the law for all people and to resist all forms of dictatorship and regimes based on violence.

The construction of the memorial began in April 2003. After the first of the stelae had been erected, the so-called Degussa debate on the graffiti-proofing of the stelae took place that October, leading to a four-week building freeze. The topping-out ceremony for the underground Information Centre took place on July 12 of the following year and the final stele was set in place on December 15, 2004. On May 12, 2005 the Memorial to the Murdered Jews of Europe was opened to the public as Germany's central Holocaust memorial. Since its inauguration, the Field of Stelae has become one of the most important sights of Berlin and the Information Centre attracts almost half a million visitors per year, making it one of the most-visited exhibitions in the German capital.

capital, Bonn. Following a lively debate, a majority of delegates from all parties approved the construction of the Holocaust Memorial according to Peter Eisenman's design and with the addition of an information centre. According to the parliamentary resolution, the memorial is intended to

An audience of 300,000 watch a new production of the rock opera "The Wall" by the former Pink Floyd member Roger Waters on the former "death strip", July 21, 1990.

THE INFORMATION CENTRE – THE EXHIBITION

Introduction

Six large illuminated portraits can be seen from the lobby of the Information Centre. These portraits represent the approximately six million murdered European Jews: men and women of different ages and backgrounds who were killed by Germans and their helpers. The narrow space containing the portraits leads to the next four exhibition rooms and the additional foyers of the Information Centre. The portraits show that the exhibition is primarily concerned with personal histories and accounts, whilst the texts and photographs on the walls provide an introduction to the history of the crimes.

At first glance it is apparent that the exhibition does not provide a detailed history of anti-semitism in Europe since the Middle Ages or of the co-existence of Jews and non-Jews in Germany and its neighbouring European countries. Instead, the narrative starts with the period after the National Socialists assumed power in Germany in January 1933. Jews were now viewed as foreigners in their own country and persecution measures against them were progressively intensified. The process was characterised by an interplay between state regulations, violence on the part of supporters of the regime and incitement by the National Socialist press. This phase of the persecution culminated in the November pogroms of 1938, when some 100 Jews were murdered by National Socialists and their sympathisers, over 1,200 synagogues destroyed and around 30,000 Jewish men put in concentration camps.

The Second World War began in September 1939 with the Wehrmacht invading Poland. It marked the start of the German policy of persecuting and murdering the Jewish

minorities in many states. Poland, a heartland of Jewish culture in Europe, was to suffer the highest number of Jewish victims. The actions of the German occupying forces in Poland had a decisive impact on the further course of the crimes in most European countries. It was in Poland that the National Socialists first forced Jews to move into separate residential areas, the so-called ghettos. Ghetto residents were stripped of their livelihoods, deployed as forced labourers and suffered from a lack of food.

1941 was to be a pivotal year for the extermination policy. For the German leaders, the war against the Soviet Union, which began on June 22, 1941, was not a military conflict fought according to the principles of international law but an ideological struggle. The aim was to eradicate the communist enemy along with their supposed communist allies, the Jews. In June 1941, SS-Einsatzgruppen (mobile killing units) began to shoot Jewish men, and from the late

Łomaży (Poland), August 18, 1942. Members of the Hamburg Reserve Police Battalion 101 herded all Jewish residents of the town into a sports field. The men and women were separated and had to sit on the ground for hours in the blazing sun.

summer Jewish women and children as well. These crimes marked the transition to genocide. By autumn 1941, the situation in the ghettos had become much worse. More and more people were dying from starvation or epidemics. In these desperate and increasingly violent conditions, the ghetto residents organised school lessons for their children along with cultural events and their own press. The German occupiers viewed the misery that they themselves had created in the ghettos as a "problem" and attempted to resolve it with violence. In the process, they developed an approach based on supposed practical necessity: the more the conditions worsened the more brutal they became. In summer 1941, the occupying forces in Poland began to make preparations for the mass murder of the Jewish population using poison gas. Heinrich Himmler, Reichsführer-SS and head of the German police, approved these plans. In December 1941, an SS commando began murdering Jews using exhaust

Jewish men are forced to dig trenches in nearby woodland. Germans and Ukrainian auxiliary police later shot 1,700 Jews. A German policeman took photographs and passed these round the members of the battalion so that they could order copies.

17

In May 1944, the SS deported around 15,000 Jews from the then Hungarian town of Munkács to Auschwitz-Birkenau. The photo shows Gerti Mermelstein together with her sister, mother and grandmother in a forest in front of the gas chamber prior to their murder.

fumes at a base near the village of Chełmno (German: Kulmhof). The victims came from the surrounding area and from the Lodz ghetto. A total of 150,000 to 320,000 Jews and 4,300 "gypsies" from the Austrian province of Burgenland were murdered.

In the first half of 1942, the German leaders started to commit genocide on a new scale. German SS and police units rounded up Jews in Polish towns and deported them to Belzec. The deportees were murdered in the gas chambers on arrival. In spring 1942, the SS constructed two further extermination camps in the Polish villages of Sobibor and Treblinka. By the time that all three extermination camps had been destroyed the following year, around 1.75 million people had died there, most of them Polish Jews. In January 1942, leading members of the NSDAP and senior civil servants had agreed on the procedure for deporting Jews from throughout Europe at a meeting in the Wannsee district of Berlin. Auschwitz-Birkenau was to become a symbol of the genocide. In spring 1942, Jews were deported here from France, Slovakia and the Third Reich, later from southern

Europe, and from spring 1944 also from Hungary. All prisoners not deployed as forced labourers were murdered in the gas chambers on arrival. By 1945, around a million European Jews had been murdered at Auschwitz, along with up to 75,000 Polish prisoners, around 21,000 Sinti und Roma, 15,000 Soviet prisoners of war and at least 10,000 prisoners from other countries.

The final section of this part of the exhibition describes the final months of the National Socialist regime in central Europe. Many prisoners lost their lives during the so-called death marches from camps in Eastern Europe to Reich territory. Thousands were also to die after liberation by the Allies as a result of their incarceration in the camps. Among these victims was Claire Brodzki, the girl featured in one of the portraits in the entrance foyer. She died on June 17, 1945, over a month after the end of the war.

The Room of Dimensions

Warsaw, November 1940: A week after the ghetto had been closed off from the outside world, some of its residents gathered in the apartment of the historian Dr Emanuel Ringelblum. They decided to found a clandestine archive and called their group "Oneg Shabbat" ("In Celebration of Sabbath") as they always met on a Saturday evening at the end of the Sabbath. Their aim was to obtain as much accurate information as possible on the crimes of the German occupation administration in Poland, and indeed they succeeded in getting information from other ghettos and later even from the extermination camps. Some of the information was typed up and published in underground newspapers. Shortly before the destruction of the ghetto the workers in the archive buried the documents stored in milk cans. Some of these were found after the war. Emanuel Ringelblum survived the liquidation of the Warsaw ghetto but was shot dead by Germans in 1944. Among the reports sent to the Warsaw ghetto was a postcard written in Polish and sent

from the Kutno ghetto in western Poland, which was then part of the "Warthegau", an administrative district annexed to the Third Reich.

"Kutno, Jan 27, 42
My dear ones!
I have already written a card to you on the fate that has befallen us. They are taking us to Chełmno and gassing us. 25,000 Jews are lying there already. The slaughter goes on. Have you no pity for us? Natan, the child, mother and I have escaped, no one else. I don't know what will become of us, I have no strength to live any more. If Aunt Bronia writes, write to her about everything. I send you warmest greetings, Fela"

Fela's identity is unclear. The clandestine communist newspaper "Morgnfrajhajt" published her text on February 9, 1942. If they were not already aware of what was happening, readers now learnt about the mass murders using gas being carried out in Chełmno, a village near Lodz. It was here that an SS commando established the first camp in occupied Poland with the purpose of systematically murdering Jews. Eyewitness testimony has provided details about what the perpetrators did here. The victims had to undress in the manor house – they were told that they had to have a wash – and then they had to get into a lorry. During the journey to a nearby forest, exhaust fumes were pumped into the windowless hold of the vehicle, with the result that those inside suffered a horrible death by suffocation. The murders began on December 8, 1941.

Around six months later, Judith Wischnjatskaja, a twelve year-old girl, wrote the following lines from Byten near Baranowicze in what was then eastern Poland (now Belarus).

"31 July 1942
Dear Father! I am saying goodbye to you before I die.
We would so love to live, but they won't let us and we will die.
I am so scared of this death, because the small children are thrown alive into the pit. Goodbye forever. I kiss you tenderly.
Your J."

21

Judith obviously wrote this farewell note just before being shot. How could she have known what was to happen to her? The SS Einsatzgruppen, German police and local auxiliaries had developed a specific system to murder people. The crimes generally took place outside the villages. The victims were forced to stand on the edge of a pit and were shot row by row. Each row was shot in front of or within earshot of the others. Historians have established that 1,900 Jews were murdered in Byten in July 1942. Judith was presumably one of the victims of this crime.

The above note, which was written alongside a Yiddish letter from Judith's mother, was found by a member of the Red Army after Byten was recaptured by the Soviets. It was translated and put into the "Black Book", a post-war publication in which Soviet intellectuals documented the atrocities carried out by the German occupying forces. On the page

(приписка по польски)

Дорогой отец! Прощаюсь с тобой перед смертью. Нам очень хочется жить, но пропало - не дают. Я так этой смерти боюсь, потому что малых детей бросают живыми в могилу. Прощайте навсегда. Целую тебя крепко, крепко.

Твоя И.

with the translation it can be seen that the original translation of Judith's Polish letter into Russian has been altered by hand. In Judith's sentence: *"… the little children are being thrown alive into the pits"*, the word "pit" (yama) was changed to "grave" (mogila). It is possible that the editors considered the word "pit" to be too degrading.

The notes from Fela and Judith are displayed in the Room of Dimensions along with thirteen further testimonies. These documents represent the few surviving messages sent out by those threatened with death at the time. They illustrate how the victims dealt with the extent of the terror.

Judith and Fela are two of the up to six million victims of the Holocaust. Only traces of their lives and what happened to them remain. We do not have the names, let along testimonies or photos, of a further three million men and women. It will thus always only be possible to establish an approximate number of those who disappeared or were murdered. Academic research has estimated that between 5.4 and six million Jews met a violent death in National Socialist dominated Europe through poison gas, mass shootings, starvation or forced labour. However, the accuracy of these estimations varies. Whilst the authorities often produced lists of names of the victims to be deported from western, northern and southern Europe, the extermination process in the East quickly claimed hundreds of thousands of lives. The perpetrators deliberately removed evidence of the murdered and their lives; documents were mainly destroyed or went missing during the war. Figures are based on documents produced by the perpetrators and lists of statistics in the countries concerned, but there are gaps in this information. The twenty states in 1937 represent 31 countries in today's Europe. Following the "annexation" of Austria in March 1938, the borders of Europe were constantly changing up to 1944–45 – especially in Eastern and Southern Europe – and so the Information Centre uses the year 1937 as the basis for its calculations.

To give one example, the Information Centre states that between 270,000 and 300,000 Jews were murdered in Hungary. Many visitors consider that this figure is too low – the

GBL Ost Berlin
PW 113 Bfsv
vom 16.1.1943

U m l a u f p l a n

für

die mehrfach zu verwendenden Wagenzüge
zur Bedienung der Sdz für Vd, Rm, Po, Pj u Da-Umsiedler
in der Zeit vom 20.1. - 18.2.1943

1	2	3	4	5	6	7
			bedient			
Uml Nr	Wagenzug der RBD	am	Zug-Nr	von	nach	Zahl der Reisenden
121	Pan 21 C	5/6.2.	Pj 107	Bialystok 9.00	Auschwitz 7.57	2000
		7/8.2.	Lp 108	Auschwitz	Bialystok	
		9.2.	Pj 127	Bialystok 9.00	Treblinka 12.10	2000
		9.2.	Lp 128	Treblinka 21.18	Bialystok 1.30	
		11.2.	Pj 131	Bialystok 9.00	Treblinka 12.10	2000
		11.2.	Lp 132	Treblinka 21.18	Bialystok 1.30	
		13.2.	Pj 135	Bialystok 9.00	Treblinka 12.10	2000
		13.2.	Lp 136	Treblinka 21.18	Bialystok 1.30	

27819

number usually given is at least 600,000. The difference can be explained by the fact that at the time of the deportations to Auschwitz-Birkenau in 1944 Hungary also included Serbian, Romanian and Slovakian territories that had been annexed after 1938. Deportees from these territories are counted as citizens of Yugoslavia, Romania and Czechoslovakia in the Room of Dimensions.

Only the central part of today's Poland matches the territory belonging to the country between 1920 and 1939. In 1937, the Polish state also included many regions that were to belong to Stalin's Soviet Union between 1939 and 1941 and after 1944–45 and are now part of the Ukraine, Belarus and Lithuania. With more than 3.1 million murdered Jews, Poland was the country with the highest number of victims, among them Judith and Fela. Around a tenth of the Polish

"Operations schedule" of the German Reichsbahn (Reich Railways) for four trains deporting 8,000 Jews from the Białystok ghetto to the Treblinka and Auschwitz extermination camps, as well as for the return of the empty carriages.

Jews survived, some as refugees in the Soviet Union. In the neighbouring countries of Latvia and Lithuania the number of survivors was even lower: between 95 and almost 100 percent of the pre-war Jewish population was murdered. Germany lost around 35 percent of its pre-1933 Jewish population (over 160,000 people). Although Jewish communities have started to flourish again in Germany since the end of the war, especially since the transformation process in 1989–90, most Polish survivors left Poland after the war, often having no other choice. For Poland and broad areas of Europe, especially Eastern Europe, the "breach in civilisation" represented by the Holocaust marked the complete eradication of a vivid culture that had existed for centuries. Barely anything remains of this culture apart from dilapidated synagogues and deserted, often ruined graveyards.

The Room of Families

"I cried for two days after receiving the letter. Something welled up inside me. After I had dried my tears, I wrote back and offered my help. […] Why me? Yes, I had already asked myself that question but I thought no more about it."

Sydney, Australia, April 2003: Sabina van der Linden, née Haberman, proprietor of a business that imports Scandinavian design products, had just received a letter from Berlin. The letter concerned her childhood in Europe or, to be more accurate, in Poland during World War Two. Over the past few years, Sabina had been dealing more intensively with the time when she and her family were persecuted and facing mortal danger as Jews. She had spoken to school classes in Australia and she had given an interview on her life to the American "Shoah Foundation". However, this was something different to the previous projects. A national Memorial to the Murdered Jews of Europe was to be established in Berlin. An employee of the foundation of the same name had come

across photos in the USA that Sabina had made available to archives. The photos showed her happy childhood in her home town of Boryslaw in the Polish region of Galicia, trips to the Carpathian Mountains and group meetings of young Zionists, but also the struggle for survival under the German occupation. It quickly became apparent that the story of the Habermans could be one of the family biographies to be displayed in the Information Centre. In the course of the subsequent collaboration with Sabina it emerged that she had kept hold of further valuable documents. She had, for example, managed to rescue parts of her diary. An entry from January 20, 1943, her brother's birthday, illustrates the situation at the time:

"We tried hard to be in a good mood, but is was very forced. I couldn't stop thinking about our mother not even for a moment… […]. – The memory of the past, the pain of our life as it is now, the hopelessness, living like animals from day to day, from 'Aktion' to 'Aktion', just to survive, just to make it through one more time. […]."

Boryslaw, January 20, 1943. Sabina Haberman (centre) and her brother Josef (first on right) with their friends Imek Eisenstein (second from right), Ducek Egit (second from left) and Rolek Hamelin (first on left). The armbands with the Jewish star are clearly visible. All Jews in Boryslaw had to wear these armbands on the orders of the German occupation forces.

In August 1942 Sabina, then 16 years old, saw her mother for the last time. Sala was deported by train to the extermination camp at Belzec along with around 4,000 other Jews from Boryslaw. The deportees were murdered on arrival with exhaust fumes from looted Soviet armoured vehicles. Despite the ongoing murders, the remaining Jews from Boryslaw must have retained the hope that the German occupiers would need them as labour reserves. After all, there were large oil reserves in the area, which were being exploited by a German company. However, in July 1942 Reichsführer SS Heinrich Himmler had issued the order for all Jewish forced labourers in the Generalgouvernement (General Government), which also included Boryslaw, to be replaced with non-Jews. The Jewish workers were to be murdered. Of the 14,000 Jews living in Boryslaw in 1941, around 4,900 remained by mid-October 1942. Around 1,200 of these were deported to Belzec on October 23 and 24, 1942, whilst others were shot dead on November 20. At the end of November, a deportation transport took a further 2,000 Jews

Berlin, May 2005. Sabina van der Linden-Wolanski, née Haberman, (centre) with her daughter Josephine, her son Phillip (partly hidden) and her grandson Remy Dennis.

from Boryslaw to Belzec. Berthold Beitz, the local oil company representative and later one of the most influential industrialists in the Federal Republic, was able to save a few Jews from deportation. Between 1941 and 1944 Beitz and his wife repeatedly attempted to save Jews, sometimes by hiding them in their house. Sabina, her brother and her friends also tried to find a safe place to stay and, like many others, sought refuge in the woods. They constantly had to weigh up the risk of living under German control against the deprivation and dangers associated with a life in hiding.

Many aspects of the persecution can no longer be explained. For example, Sabina is in the dark about the events that happened prior to July 19, 1944. On that day, her brother, her father and her boyfriend Mendzio Dörfler were shot dead by a firing squad in the camp grounds. Sabina was now completely alone. Later she learnt that her brother had previously left a forced labour unit in neighbouring Stryj. What was his intention? Sabina only found out about the murder two days later when she left her hiding place in the woods to go to Boryslaw. Prior to this she had apparently only narrowly missed being discovered herself. On August 7, 1944 the Red Army entered Boryslaw. This marked a new phase in the life of the Polish Jewess Sabina Haberman. The town became part of the Ukrainian Soviet Socialist Republic. Like many Jewish survivors, Sabina ended up in what used to be the German territory of Lower Silesia and she then moved westwards to Paris. However, she found happiness much further away in Australia, the country which she emigrated to in 1950.

When Sabina visited her home town in 1993 she met two Jewish men who still lived there. When she returned in 2006 they were gone. The Boryslaw of her youth no longer exists. Jewish life has disappeared from Galicia. The Information Centre aims also at remembering these cultural losses. The Room of Families evokes the destruction of the diversity of Jewish life in Europe. Some of the 15 families depicted had similar traditions even though they lived far away from each other. For example, the Hofman family (from a Paris suburb) and the Turteltaub family (from near Lake Constance) both had Polish Jewish origins. Others continued to observe regional customs in their home towns, for example the David family, whose history in Greece dated back to the Roman period of rule. By contrast, the Demajos family from Belgrade belonged to the world of Sephardic Jewry; the culture of Jews who were expelled from Spain and Portugal in the 15th and 16th century and found refuge in the Netherlands, North German and Italy, but especially the Balkans. Up until the 20th century they continued to speak their own language, Ladino. The desire of the German occupiers to exterminate the Jews also affected the Sephardic Jews and their culture from Amsterdam to Hamburg and from Saloniki to Belgrade. All of the Jews living in Serbia were targeted by National Socialist extermination policy from April 1941. Most of the Jewish men fell victim to mass shooting operations carried out by the Wehrmacht in autumn 1941.

In spring 1942, the SS went on to murder the Jewish women and children in so-called gas trucks that travelled through Belgrade. Almost all of the Demajo family had died by May 1942. Among the dead was the sister of Lili Varon, née Pijade, who has loaned the family photos shown in this room.

In 2003, Lili's elderly brother, Dr Rafael Pijade, responded to an appeal in the newspaper of the Jewish community in Belgrade and provided his photographs. Rafael Pijade was still alive when the Memorial to the Murdered Jews of Europe opened in May 2005 (he died two years later). As he was no longer able to travel to Berlin, his granddaughter went to the opening ceremony in his place. The members of the families shown in this room visited the exhibition a day before its official inauguration. They spent a long time looking at the illuminated stelae. It was then that the Room of Families attained its most personal meaning: *"Our grandfather and aunt now finally have a gravestone."*

Belgrade, 1924. Members of the Demajo, Arueti and Elkalay families at a picnic. The photo was kept by relatives who fled to Bulgaria in 1943.

The Room of Names

In the dimly-lit Room of Names there are small illuminated seating areas where visitors can listen to voices recounting the story of individual Jews and the destruction of Jewish communities. The names and, if known, the places of birth and death of these persons are projected onto the walls. Research was carried out into the lives of over 10,000 Jewish men, women and children for this part of the exhibition, with the generous support of the Association Memorial to the Murdered Jews of Europe. One would need to spend around six years, seven months and 27 days in the Room of Names in order to hear the names and biographies of all the murdered and missing Jews listed here. And yet not even the names are known of half the victims of the Holocaust. The names that are known have been found, often barely legible, on transport lists and other documents produced by the perpetrators.

   In many cases, relatives or friends began trying to trace the whereabouts of the missing directly after the war. For

Missing persons advert, Aufbau newspaper, November 2, 1945.

example, they placed adverts in "Aufbau", the biggest selling German-language newspaper for exiles in the USA. Kurt Ehrlich, born in 1883 in Frankfurt (Oder), and his Viennese wife

Stella, who was ten years younger, were deported from their home in Berlin to the Auschwitz-Birkenau extermination camp on May 17, 1943. The SS murdered them on arrival using Zyklon B gas. By the time that the advert was placed they had been dead for two years, but their daughter had no idea what had happened to them – and possibly never found out during her lifetime. In any case, she was not among the hundreds of thousands to fill out a page of testimony for the Yad Vashem memorial site in Israel.

The National Socialist regime produced reams of paperwork pertaining to German Jews in order to make the murders seem like a completely standard bureaucratic process. Whilst many of these documents still exist, there are few such files related to Jews from Eastern Europe. In the case of the Polish Waintraub family, all that remains are the handwritten pages of testimony from a Jewish relative. This relative is their son, who now lives in Israel by the name of Avraham Gafni. He has submitted all that he knows about his family to Yad Vashem. However, it is still impossible to ascertain what happened to his mother and sister. It is difficult to conduct research in former Polish territories. Almost half of the over six million Jewish victims in Europe came from Poland. Hence, half of the biographies in the Room of Names concern Polish Jews.

In 1942, a ghetto was established in the Waintraub family's home town, Międzyrzec Podlaski, the name of which is barely pronounceable for non-Poles. The town was conveniently placed between Warsaw and Brest-Litowsk, with a train line linking the two. In 1942–43 it was, after Izbica, the largest transit ghetto in the Lublin district. This district was part of the General Government, the central site of the Holocaust. Jews from Poland, Slovakia and other West European states were confined in the ghetto before being murdered at Treblinka. Of the approximately 16,000 Jews living in Międzyrzec Podlaski (around 75 percent of the total population), up to 2,000 of the young residents were able to escape to the Soviet Union at the beginning of the Second World War in autumn 1939. Of those who remained behind, 170 survived. Among them was Avraham Gafni, whose father had made him jump from the train travelling to Treblinka. He hid

Jews forced to assemble on the market place in Międzyrzec Podlaski were made to kneel down until their deportation. Anyone who moved was shot by the SS and their Ukrainian auxiliaries. This photo from 1943 was probably taken in secret.

The memorial stone arrives at the market place. In the front of the photo (shown from behind) is the sculptor Yael Artzi, who gave her sculpture the title "Prayer". The photo was taken by Naphtali Brezniak, the son of a Holocaust survivor, in May 2009.

in the surrounding forests and spent the winter in a wooden shed of the forester Piotr Ulandsky. He was the only member of his family to survive.

Avraham's home town is well known to researchers. In the 1960s, some of the members of the reserve police battalion 101 were put on trial in Hamburg and there is thus

extensive information about the perpetrators. Yet strangely the history of these "ordinary men" (to use the title of the famous book by the historian Christopher Browning) who became mass murderers in the Lublin district does not include details on the victims. There are now lists of names of those murdered in many Polish villages and small towns, but not for Międzyrzec Podlaski, and so no such list could be used to compile the related audio materials in the Room of Names.

The Foundation Memorial to the Murdered Jews of Europe succeeded in making contact with Avraham Gafni, formerly known as Gad Finkelstein, who as a teenager had managed to escape the raids and murders. Contact was also established with some of the relatives of survivors in Israel, who had apparently already spent years looking into the forgotten history of their home towns. These relatives, who have found an association of immigrants originating from Międzyrzec, worked closely with the Foundation. They had already acquired the information that the Foundation researches in order to produce audio materials for the Room of Names. Hence, they had gathered biographical information, checked the spelling of names and compared historical data with the academic literature and the archive materials they had collected over the years. Moreover, they had scanned photos, conducted comparative research to identify individuals and translated the biographies into English. The only thing left to do in Berlin was to produce the audio materials using this information.

Information was exchanged by email over a period of several months. There were meetings between those involved in the project and the group was invited to Poland. The research that the group carried out for the Room of Names, which presents biographies of their relatives in audio format, ultimately led them back to the home towns of those who were murdered. In Poland, the group wanted to erect a memorial to their relatives and to the entire Jewish population of Międzyrzec in the large market square in the town centre. The town council eventually understood the reasons for establishing the memorial in this location. Most of the houses and businesses belonging to Jewish families had formerly been on this square, but the square was also used by the perpetrators to assemble Jews prior to deportations. For Avraham Gafni this was the only conceivable site for the memorial. He still has horrific memories of the first major "operation" in August 1942, when the police battalion 101 deported 10,000 people in 52 cattle cars in the space of two days: *It was a hot summer's day. After two long days hiding in a dark place I was blinded by the sun. There were hundreds of*

bodies lying in pools of dried blood on the square and flies everywhere. I will never be able to forget this image as long as I live." The memorial is a sculpture of a person deep in prayer. The inauguration took place in the presence of residents of the town as well as 125 people from Israel, the USA, England, Canada and Australia with family links to the town, most of whom had never seen each other before.

In the Room of Names visitors can hear the story of Avraham Gafni's mother:
"Gittle Waintraub was born on November 10, 1897 in Międzyrzec Podlaski. She owned a prosperous hairdressing salon with a staff of six. After German troops occupied the Polish town in 1939, the occupiers robbed Gittle Waintraub of her livelihood. On May 26, 1943, men from the Hamburg reserve police battalion 101 forced Gittle Waintraub and her five year-old daughter into a train going to the Treblinka extermination camp. She probably jumped from the train with her daughter in her arms. There has been no trace of Gittle Waintraub since."

Avraham Gafni's mother, Gittle Waintraub.

Auschwitz-Birkenau

Babij Jar

Sobibor

Malyj Trostenez

The Room of Sites

Belzec is a small village in the south-east of today's Poland, over 900 kilometres from Berlin. To get there from Berlin, one takes the motorway towards Dresden, passing Cottbus and Wrocław. Starting at Cracow, once seat of the Polish kings, practically every town and village along this route witnessed National Socialist crimes, primarily against Polish Jews. Towards the east is the now Ukrainian city of L'viv. In Polish it was known as Lwów, in German: Lemberg. The city used to be the capital of Galicia, a significant cultural landscape of the Habsburg Empire. This region is now divided between Poland and the Ukraine. The tragedy to befall Lwów's Jewish population, which numbered over 100,000, as well as the thousands of small towns and villages in Galicia, is closely linked with Belzec. Between 1939–41 and 1944 Galicia was part of the General Government, the area of conquered Poland that fell directly under German administration and that was to become the epicentre of the German policy of violence and extermination.

From Rzeszów onwards, the route to Belzec is via bumpy, narrow country roads. There are sparse forests and vast meadows with the occasional farm and village, whose only decorative feature used to be the Catholic church and the synagogue. Most of the synagogues have disappeared or are empty; the Jewish population is gone. Belzec is on a trainline that used to go from Lublin to Lemberg. On the orders of Odilo Globocnik, the senior SS and police leader in the Lublin district, the first of three extermination camps built to murder the local Jewish population was established next to Belzec station at the end of 1941. Belzec is also situated by a main road. Belzec was not a camp – no one stayed here. It was rather a death factory the size of a building supplies store. The mass murder of 450,000 to 600,000 Jews from eastern Galicia – the area including Lublin, Cracow and Lemberg – was carried out over the course of just eight months in 1942. It was not concealed from the outside world but was part of everyday life. The SS members responsible subsequently destroyed and levelled the site and planted trees and crops.

39

Deportation from the Rzeszów ghetto to the Belzec gas chambers, 1942.

Decades later in the 1970s, the local resident Wacław Kołodziejczyk painted two pictures, one of which was an "Overview of the Belzec Death Camp". This picture shows a crowd of people getting off a train, guards with dogs and a person addressing the arrivals – the usual procedure adopted to dupe the deportees. They were told that they were there to work and just had to have a shower beforehand. The German SS and their Ukrainian helpers subsequently murdered the Jewish men, women and children using exhaust fumes. Their death by suffocation lasted twenty to thirty minutes. Within a few months entire areas had been stripped of their population and the region lost centuries of Polish-Jewish identity. The Reichsbahn (the German railways) transported suitcases, clothes, jewellery and gold fillings back to Germany.

Kołodziejczyk's paintings are in the vicarage in Belzec. Attempts to reproduce the one picture for the exhibition in Berlin failed initially, despite local support. After the bishop of the nearby district town of Zamość had agreed to loan the painting "Overview of the Belzec Death Camp" to the exhibition, a representative from the Foundation travelled to Belzec to collect it. Dagmar von Wilcken, the curator of the exhibition in the Information Centre, was sceptical: *"It's awful! Is there nothing else?"* However, this naïve painting is also a record of the Holocaust and practically the only evidence of the camp. Belzec was one of the three extermination sites established in the General Government under "Operation Reinhardt". The other two – Sobibor and Treblinka

Wacław Kołodziejczyk
"Overview of the Belzec Death Camp", 1970s.

OGÓLNY WIDOK OBOZU ŚMIERCI W BEŁŻCU.

FRAGMENT WYŁADOWANIA LUDZI Z WAGONÓW PRZEZNACZONYCH NA ŚMIERĆ. OBÓZ CZYNNY BYŁ OD M-CA MARCA 1942r. DO WIOSNY 1943r. W TYM CZASIE PRZYWIEZIONO OKOŁO JEDNEGO MILJONA OSIEMSET TYSIĘCY LUDZI I UŚMIERCONO W SPECJALNEJ KOMORZE GAZOWEJ. ŻYD NAZWISKIEM IRMANN, KTÓRY W PROWADZIE DO KOMORY GAZOWEJ 23 OSOBY ZE SWOJEJ NAJBLIŻSZEJ RODZINY, W TYM I SWOJĄ NARZECZONĄ, I ZAWSZE PRZEMAWIAŁ KRÓTKO: "IHR GEHTS JETZT BADEN, NACHHER WERDET IHR ZUR ARBEIT GESBICKT" (TERAZ BĘDZIE KĄPIEL, A POTEM BĘDZIECIE PRZYDZIELANI DO PRACY).

Belzec after 1944. From left to right: the station, platforms, warehouse and grounds of the extermination site.

– are, like Belzec, virtually unknown. Between May 1942 and June 1943, the SS murdered around 250,000 Polish, German, Dutch, French, Lithuanian and Belarussian Jews at Sobibor. Between July 1942 and May 1943, around 2,000 Roma and 800,000 to 900,000 Jews – all but a few from Poland – died at Treblinka. There are no photos, apart from aerial shots taken by the German Luftbildstaffel (aerial photograph unit) in spring 1944 which show all three death sites after they had been destroyed and levelled. Up to 1.75 million people died at these three extermination sites, almost a third of the total number of Holocaust victims.

Lubny is 180 kilometres east of the Ukrainian capital Kiev. Most of the Jews from Lubny were able to escape before the invasion of the German Werhmacht in September 1941. Following the arrival of military troops, mobile SS units swept through the conquered Soviet territories that autumn. In late autumn 1941, the local German commander I/922 ordered the Jews in Lubny to assemble on October 16 at 9 am. He claimed that they were to be "resettled" and therefore had to bring enough provisions for three days and warm clothing. The Jews were grouped together in a field cordoned off by the security forces. They had to hand over their luggage and undress before being led off to be shot in groups by members of Sonderkommando (special commando) 4a of SS Einsatzgruppe C, under the orders of SS Standartenführer (colonel) Paul Blobel. There are 33 existing photographs of this execution, taken by Johannes Hähle from the Propadanda

Members of Sonderkommando (special commando) 4 a of the SS Einsatzgruppe C (a mobile killing unit) carry out a mass shooting of 1,865 Jewish men, women and children from Lubny, October 16, 1941.

Unit 637 of the Sixth Army. They show Jews on the way to the extermination site and above all hundreds of people waiting in a field dressed in warm, very basic clothing. These include a mother with a child sleeping in her arms and her son holding something to eat in his hand, a young couple, and a grandfather with his grandson. Their eyes are full of fear and despondency. There is also a picture of a little girl of around three or four years old, wearing a white scarf around her head and dressed in an oversized army jacket. She is looking directly into the camera with a questioning, inquisitive, almost cheeky expression. This and other photos from the series are among the most powerful visual testimonies of the Holocaust. According to their own calculations, the SS and their local helpers shot 1,865 Jewish men, women and children on October 16, 1941. The German commandant's headquarters in Lubny seized their valuables and abandoned property; non-Jewish Ukrainians also helped themselves to these items. What happened in Lubny was repeated over and over again behind the Eastern front – from Polangen on the Baltic Sea in Lithuania to Odessa on the Black Sea in the Ukraine. Around two million Jews fell victim to mass shootings. In many places, non-Jewish children aged between six and nine from farming families were forced to witness and indeed to carry out horrendous tasks before, during and after the execution of their Jewish neighbours and classmates. They had to fill in pits where people

Lubny, October 16, 1941.

were still moving because a substantial number of victims were merely shot at and babies were thrown alive into the pits of murdered people. They were exploited as "tampers", having to tread down on the bodies and then sprinkle them with sand so that the next group of Jews could lie down "more easily" before being shot.

Belzec and Lubny are just two of thousands of places where the National Socialist genocide was perpetrated throughout Europe. Murders took place in the gas chambers in the death camps, in countless mass shooting pits in forests in Poland, Lithuania, Latvia, Romania, Belarus and the Ukraine, as well as in hundreds of cordoned-off ghetto districts. Millions of Jews and non-Jews met a violent death in deportation trains and mobile gas vans, during pogroms and "reprisal operations" and in concentration and forced labour camps. 220 of these largely unknown sites of terror are shown in the Room of Sites.

Lubny, October 16, 1941.

Portal to the Sites of Memory in Europe

The rooms in the Information Centre evoke a particular atmosphere. Although visitors are not asked to remain silent, there is an air of almost solemn calmness in the darkened rooms, even with large numbers of visitors. Each room feels different. Visitors bend down to read the personal accounts in the Room of Dimensions, but in the Room of Sites they look upwards at the pictures and text providing information about the places where the genocide took place. A map of Europe displayed at the exit of this final room of the Centre has a real impact. The map features orange rectangles marking places where Jews and non-Jews were incarcerated, deported and murdered. The hundreds of rectangles only show the main sites of National Socialist terror; if all of the sites were featured the map would be almost completely orange. The concentration of sites in Eastern Europe is particularly striking.

When visitors leave the Room of Sites, they are brought back to the present in two ways. First, their eyes have to get used to the daylight after being in the dark rooms. Some visitors sit on the benches in the brightly-lit foyer and pupils sit waiting for their classmates. They have time to take a break but also to gradually reflect on what they have just seen, read and heard. The main question that arises is what Europe remembers of these horrific events and how they are commemorated. The virtual portal to sites of memory aims to respond to this question. This portal also features a map of Europe showing sites of memory. There is again a difference between both sides of the map, but this time the majority of sites marked are on the left, in Western Europe. Western Europe has countless museums and memorial sites, whereas Eastern Europe mainly has memorials. However, this imbalance is gradually disappearing as there is a constant evolution in both how remembrance is shaped and what is being remembered.

One example is Belzec in Poland. After practically all of the Jews from the area between Cracow, Lublin and Lemberg had been murdered at Belzec, the SS proceeded to erase all traces of the crime. The human remains were crushed and disposed of and the camp grounds were turned into a farm. Nothing changed for decades until the authorities of the People's Republic of Poland put up a memorial with the inscription "In memory of the victims of Hitlerite terror murdered from 1942–43". As with the state memorial at Auschwitz, the Polish state did not consider it necessary to name the victims as Jews. It would be wrong to assume that Belzec was forgotten after the war, instead, it had never been present in the public consciousness. The collapse of the Soviet-style dictatorships in Central and Eastern Europe meant that free and public discussion was possible after decades where silence and repressed memory had prevailed. Two decades after the events of 1989–90 the legacy of the past is a key topic for debate. Such debates are difficult enough in other countries, as demonstrated by the examples of France, the Netherlands or Denmark, but they

Memorial site at the former Belzec extermination camp. There are still mass graves in the grounds.

are even more painful in countries such as Poland, Lithuania or the Ukraine, which were left so traumatised by the experience of German and Soviet occupation. Visitors to the former Belzec extermination camp now see an impressive memorial landscape. It was initiated and financed by the

Memorial at the IX. Fort in Kaunas (Lithuania), where mass shootings took place between 1941 and 1944.

American Jewish Committee. A long path or 'tube' cuts through the grounds to show the final route taken by the victims, becoming deeper and deeper. This is no abstract site: there are mass graves throughout the grounds. The sheer horror of the site is almost tangible, but also its ab-

surdity. The adjacent museum primarily charts the places where the murdered Jews came from.

There are barely any traces of the places where the mass shootings of European Jews were carried out, especially those following the German invasion of the Soviet Union in summer 1941. The Jewish population was largely wiped out in most of these places and it was not easy for any survivors to preserve the memory of those who had died. The Soviet authorities removed Stars of David and inscriptions in Hebrew or at best they replaced them with Russian-language inscriptions mentioning "peaceful Soviet citizens who became victims of fascism". That, too, has changed by now. There are now hundreds of memorial stones – often in very remote locations – in the area between the Baltic Sea and the Black Sea, thus highlighting the vast geographical dimensions of the Holocaust. Although these memorials are often hidden in remote forests and hard to find, they now do exist.

The memorial site portal has a database featuring hundreds of such sites of memory and thereby gives an overview of the extremely diverse and constantly evolving cultures of memory in Europe, from the Pyrenees to the Urals, from Norway to Greece. Using the computer terminals, visitors can immediately access detailed information about what the memorials look like, when they were constructed and their historical context. They can also access practical information, for example details of how to get there. This database is constantly extended and updated.

Video Archive

For most people, the notion of an archive conjures up images of a dark and dusty place where academics work with disintegrating documents and old papers, where painstaking research is carried out to decipher dull, obscure and strange documents and where experts deal with unfamiliar and difficult concepts. Only few are familiar with how archive work is really carried out.

However, the video archive in the Information Centre is different. This archive is open to all: not only to researchers or those interested in a specific historical event or a particular town, but also to those who "just want to have a look". Visitors can sit at one of the computer terminals and listen to the accounts of Holocaust survivors through the headphones. They can listen to these for hours if they so wish, or search and select very short extracts from the lengthy accounts.

A key feature of the archive is that it is not a silent place. One can listen to people of all ages and countries speaking in many different languages. For example, there is a man born in the early 1920s in the Spandau district of Berlin who talks about his childhood and youth in true Berlin dialect. His captivating account takes the listener back to the age of the Weimar Republic. However, this boy is then deported to Auschwitz. However hard it is to listen to what he goes on to say, the listener does not feel detached from the account. This is because he speaks about Auschwitz in the same Berlin dialect. It thereby becomes clear that this boy was from the city of Berlin, that he was a friend, a neighbour, perhaps a little rascal; that he spent his daily life in Berlin, his home, and that he suddenly disappeared for no reason. If one searches in the video archive for places near one's own home town, one will encounter other survivors who speak in different dialects or languages about what happened to them.

After some time one notices that the survivors are not just speaking into a microphone and on camera but that they are addressing the listener directly. Many gave these interviews because they wanted to make their personal stories accessible to future generations, and to school pupils in particular. For this reason, they talk about everyday life – the things that happened on the way to school, trips, friends, family life – up to the point when they were torn away from all of these things.

There are naturally many things that the interviewees find very painful to talk about. Yet it is also sometimes hard for the listener to deal with what they are hearing. For example, a Jewish lady from Poland who was still a little girl during the Second World War recounts how she hid in terror behind a curtain as SS men forced their way into her parents' apartment. She listened to the Germans searching

for her and then realised that one of the intruders was approaching her hiding place. As she lay face down on the floor she could see the shiny boot of the SS man underneath the curtain with her own face reflected in it. A Jewish lady from the Netherlands, who was interviewed together with her son, recalls how she reluctantly gave him to a neighbour to be looked after following the occupation of Amsterdam. The last thing she said to him was that he would have a nice day at the zoo. She did not see him again for several years. And yet her actions saved him as both are now sitting in front of the camera, visibly moved, and talking about it.

Although it is sometimes difficult and challenging to listen to such accounts, the fact that it is the voices and faces of the survivors speaking about the Holocaust means that the video archive is a living place where everyone can hear the most personal experiences of individuals. Sitting and listening to these people and what happened to them, one begins to grasp the murderous dimensions of the Holocaust.

Ada Willenberg during an interview with the Foundation Memorial, June 2009.

Samuel Willenberg, June 2009.

It is not just the "presence" of the survivors that makes the video archive a place of active confrontation with the past. The technical features of the archive allow visitors themselves to play an active role. The videos are in digital form, which means that visitors can at any stage rewind or fast forward the interviews. If they have not understood something they can read the transcript of the interview as they watch it or they can access a translation. They can also run a search for places or people and retrieve additional historical information.

Just as the Holocaust Memorial is in many respects the opposite of what most people understand by a memorial, the video archive is the opposite of what many people understand by an archive. It is a place that one enters together with the survivors and that continues to provide new insights into the highly personal experiences of those who had to go through the Holocaust.

ADDITIONAL SERVICES AT THE INFORMATION CENTRE

Databases

The Names of Holocaust Victims from Yad Vashem

How can the names and memory of Holocaust victims be preserved and how can future generations trace branches of their family tree eradicated by the National Socialists? In 1953, the Israeli Parliament responded to these questions by founding Israel's largest national memorial site for the "Holocaust martyrs and heroes" in Jerusalem. The site is called "Yad Vashem" (after the Hebrew words "yad" for memorial and "shem" for name) and it was given the task of collecting so-called pages of testimony. These pages contain biographical information on Holocaust victims provided by relatives, friends and acquaintances. To a certain extent, they are intended to serve as a substitute for the missing gravestones of the Jews who were murdered or disappeared. They are kept in the "Hall of Names". Over two million pages of testimony have been collected so far. These also include the names of 320,000 children, who are mentioned alongside their parents. Half of the pages contain a photograph of the person. This database is gradually being expanded to include names and biographical information from other sources. Dozens of volunteers examine memorial books and lists of victims, including those deported or shot, in order to retrieve these names. Yad Vashem has thus been able to establish the name and details of the death of over 3.3 million murdered Jews so far. These sources and the close cooperation with Yad Vashem are indispensable for the Foundation, especially when it comes to extending the Room of Names.

One of the aims of Yad Vashem is to make all available sources accessible in the hope that this will lead to additional contacts, documentation and exhibitions. The pages of

YAD VASHEM
The Holocaust Martyrs' and Heroes' Remembrance Authority
Hall of Names

יד ושם
רשות הזיכרון לשואה ולגבורה
היכל השמות

Page of Testimony דף עד

דף עד לריושם והנצחה של הנספים; נא למלא דף עבור כל נספה בנפרד, בכתב בר
commemoration of the Jews who perished during the Holocaust; please fill in a separate form for each victim, in block capitals

The Martyrs' and Heroes' Remembrance Law 5713-1953 determines in section 2 that: "The task of Yad Vashem is to gather into the homeland material regarding all those members of the Jewish people who laid down their lives, who fought and rebelled against the Nazi enemy and his collaborators, and to perpetuate their **names** and those of the communities, organizations and institutions which were destroyed because they were Jewish."

Maiden name: שם משפחה של הנספה:	שם משפחה (גם שם קודם/כינוי): Victim's family name:	תואר:
ZINGER	WAINTRAUB	
Previous/other family name: שם משפחה קודם/אחר:	First name (also nickname): שם פרטי (גם שם חיבה/כינוי):	
	GITL	

Approx. age at death: גיל משוער בעת המוות:	Date of birth: תאריך לידה:	Gender: מין:	Title: תואר:	
42	1901	M (F) ז / נ		

Nationality: נתינות:	Country: ארץ:	Region: מחוז:	Place of birth: מקום לידה:
POLISH	POLAND	LUBLIN	MIEDZYRZEC PODLASKI

Victim's father:	Family name: שם משפחה:	First name: שם פרטי:	אב
	ZINGER	ABRAHAM	הנספה:

Victim's mother:	Maiden name: שם הנשואין:	First name: שם פרטי:	אם
			הנספה:

Victim's wife/husband:	No. of children: מס' ילדים:	Family status: מצב משפחתי:	Maiden name: שם הנשואין:	First name: שם פרטי:	איש/בעל(ה)
	2	MARRIED		SHLOMO	של הנספה:

Address: כתובת:	Country: ארץ:	Region: מחוז:	Permanent residence: מקום מגורים קבוע:
ul KOSCIELNA 3	POLAND	LUBLIN	MIEDZYRZEC PODLASKI

Member of org./movement: חבר בארגון/תנועה:	Place of work: מקום העבודה:	Profession: מקצוע:
	ul KOSCIELNA 3	SEAMSTRESS

Address: כתובת:	Country: ארץ:	Region: מחוז:	Residence before migration: מגורים לפני העליה:
ul KOSCIELNA 3	POLAND	LUBLIN	MIEDZYRZEC PODLASKI

אירועים / פעולות ומקומות בזמן המלחמה (מעצר / גירוש / גיטו / מחנה / עבודת מוות / ברוחה / התנגדות / לחימה):
Places, events and activities during the war (prison / deportation / ghetto / camp / death march / hiding / escape / resistance / combat):

Date of death: תאריך המוות:	Country: ארץ:	Region: מחוז:	Place of death: מקום המוות:
1943	POLAND		TREBLINKA

Circumstances of death: נסיבות המוות:

אני הח"מ, מצהיר/ה בזה כי העדות שמסרתי על פרטיו נכונה ואמיתית לפי מיטב ידיעתי והכרתי.
I, the undersigned, hereby declare that this testimony is correct to the best of my knowledge.

Previous/maiden name: שם משפחה קודם:	Family name: שם משפחה:	First name: שם פרטי:
	GITTI WAINTRAUB	ABRAHAM

State/Zip code: אזור/מיקוד:	City: עיר:	Apt.: דירה:	Entrance: כניסה:	House no.: מס' בית:	Street: רחוב:
62504	TEL-AVIV			30	SHARET

Relationship to victim (family/other): הקרבה (משפחתית/אחרת) לנספה:		Tel.: טל':	Country: מדינה:
MY MATHER	I am / I am not a survivor	03-5468541	ISRAEL

בזמן המלחמה הייתי במחנה / גטו / יער / מנסתור / בצרות בזוה / ביערות / במחתרת (הקף בעיגול).
Holocaust survivors may order a special form in which to fill in their details. During the war I was in a camp / ghetto / forest / the resistance / in hiding / had fake papers (circle relevant options)

Date: תאריך:	Place: מקום:	Signature: חתימה:
15/4/88	TEL-AVIV	

777

"ונתתי להם בביתי ובחומותי יד ושם...אשר לא יכרת" ישעיהו נ"ו ה'
"...And I shall give them in My house and within My walls a memorial and a name...that shall not be cut off" Isaiah 56:5

---

testimony, which are filled out in many different languages, can thus now be consulted via the Internet and they have been translated into English. Visitors to the exhibition in the Information Centre can access this database. They can also use it to search for information on what happened to Jews from their home town or country.

The Memorial Book of the German Federal Archives

The German Federal Archives, founded in 1952, have produced a memorial book entitled "Victims of the Persecution of Jews under National Socialist Tyranny in Germany, 1933–45". For the Federal President Horst Köhler, this book *"restores the names, and therefore the dignity, of the murdered. It is both a memorial and a reminder of the fact that every single human being has a name and a unique history."* The memorial book has been available online in the Information Centre since 2008. The current version contains the names of 159,972 Jewish men, women and children from Germany, including around 155,000 of the up to 165,000 Jews who were murdered or went missing. The

Page of testimony for Gittle Waintraub.

collection of names and biographies of victims is far from complete.

Since the first edition of the memorial book in 1986, research into new sources has been ongoing. Following the unification of East and West Germany in October 1990 and the merging of the contents of the West German Federal Archives and the Central State Archives of the GDR, it has been possible to carry out research about the victims from what are now the five new federal states in eastern Germany as well as the former eastern territories of Germany. The results of this research went into the second edition of the memorial book. Of particular significance was the census of May 17, 1939, in which the National Socialist state gathered information about people's Jewish origins – irrespective of their faith and whether or not these people considered themselves to be Jewish. This provided the Nazis with an unprecedented statistical resource to use in further depriving Jews of their rights. Additional sources related to the approximately 17,000 mainly Jewish men of Polish nationality who were deported to Poland by the Nazi regime in October 1938, as well as their

The economist Cora Berliner (*1890), after whom the postal address of the Holocaust Memorial is named. Up to a few years ago, it was merely known that she had died somewhere in Eastern Europe. It has since been established that she was deported on June 24, 1942 from Berlin via Königsberg (now Kaliningrad) to the Maly rostenets extermination site near Minsk. She was murdered there.

family members who remained behind. The latter had also been expelled by summer 1939; the authorities frequently only marked their files with the innocuous term "moved away". There were often no further traces of these people, 7,000 of whom are mentioned in the memorial book.

The Debate on the Memorial

On June 25, 1999, the German Bundestag voted to construct a Memorial to the Murdered Jews of Europe. The debates and controversies on whether and how this project should be realised lasted for many years and were crucial to the decision-making process. Moreover, they secured public awareness of the project and turned it into a citizen-led process. In this sense, the debate is already part of the memorial as a sign of active memory. For this reason, the history of the memorial is documented in the Information Centre along with the historical information and reference to other memorial sites.

At the end of October 2003 it emerged that "Protectosil", a product made by the company "Degussa", was being used to protect the concrete blocks from graffiti. The company "Degesch" (German Pest Control Company), a subsidiary of Degussa, produced the poison gas "Zyklon B" during the National Socialist period. This gas was used by the SS between 1942 and 1944 to murder in excess of one million people, most of them Jews, in the Auschwitz-Birkenau and Lublin-Majdanek camps on occupied Polish territory. The dispute over the use of "Protectosil" led to a four-week building freeze at the site. A debate raged for weeks in Germany and Europe, focusing above all on the possible conclusions to be drawn in the present from the fact that many German companies had conducted business with the Third Reich. In mid-November 2003, the board of trustees of the Foundation Memorial to the Murdered Jews of Europe, headed by the former President of the Bundestag Wolfgang Thierse, decided to continue using Degussa products in the construction of the memorial and to chart this debate in the Information Centre.

The terminal at the entrance of the Information Centre provides a broad range of information on the different

Die Holocaustmahnmalgroteske

Chemischer Antifaschismus-Test

Schuldige Steine

Schöner bauen mit Degussa

Geisel der Geschichte

Mahnmal: Droht jetzt der Abriss?

debates on the memorial. It is possible to download a large number of press articles documenting the history of the memorial project.

Visitor Service and Educational Programmes

Guten Tag! How are you? Bonjour! ¡Buenos días! שלום! Buon giorno! Добрый день! Dzień dobry! Members of the visitor service personally greet visitors in many languages. They hand out a leaflet with information on the Field of Stelae and on the exhibition in the Information Centre. The leaflet is available in 14 languages. Despite the crowds and the hustle and bustle it is apparent that each visitor is welcome and treated with respect. Their individual needs and requirements are at the heart of the work of the memorial. Visitors include Holocaust survivors who have travelled with relatives from Israel or the USA back to their home city of Berlin just to see the memorial. There are also tourists from all over the world, who often "come across" the Field of Stelae during a city tour, and a large number of school classes, groups of

soldiers or tourist parties who have pre-booked a tour or a workshop by phone.

Before visiting the memorial, many people say that they expect it *"to be very depressing"* and it is therefore the task of the visitor service to create a friendly and welcoming atmosphere where one can acquire information, exchange views and remember the victims of the Holocaust. This atmosphere gives each visitor scope to reflect on what they have seen and to engage with the personal accounts, the family biographies and the factual information. The peace and the quiet, the contemplative atmosphere in the exhibition rooms and the many positive entries in the visitor books all show that these aims have been realised. The following two comments are representative of the reactions of many foreign visitors: *"I am impressed that the German Government built this place and confronted its own past"; "German understanding of their history – impressive compared to other countries."*

The Field of Stelae offers a contrast to the calm of the Information Centre. In addition to the many visitors walking through the Field of Stelae or pausing at one of the concrete

blocks, one can also see many groups of teenagers or adults engaged in animated conversation. If these discussions take place during a guided visit of the site, they are moderated by a member of the memorial's educational staff, who can add context related to the form of the Field of Stelae and the content of the exhibition. The objective of transmitting such information is not to lecture visitors but to encourage active dialogue. Each visitor responds differently to the experience of walking through the Field of Stelae and having to find their bearings within it. The guides invite visitors to make comments and comparisons and to give their impressions of the memorial, and they discuss conflicting perspectives. They consider themselves as facilitators who take account of the specific interests and experiences of each group. In order to preserve its character as a memorial site, there are no guided visits of the Information Centre. However, the visitor service does offer a 70-minute audio tour in German or English. The audioguide explains the individual rooms in the exhibition. The curators talk about the research they carried out for the exhibition and their meetings with survivors, whose personal documents can be seen in the exhibition.

The ever-growing number of young people visiting the memorial contradicts the pessimistic view that young people are losing interest in the past. When asked which aspect of their visit to the memorial had left the greatest impression, one visitor stated in March 2009: *"All the young people who are here."* A schoolgirl summed up her emotional encounter with the testimony of a Holocaust survivor during a study day in the video archive thus: *"Willi F. sits there and talks. It is 1996. 50 years since it happened. One person can speak for the almost 1 million who never left the camps. For everyone!"* Young people have the chance to "get to know" a Holocaust survivor in the video archive and to engage with the individual stages of their lives – the experience of marginalisation, persecution and the murder of friends and relatives, but also the desire to make a new start after 1945. During the workshops, pupils go into the various themes in the exhibition in more detail by researching the sources presented along with additional materials. They attempt to imagine what things

were like at the time. What was life like for the Grossman family in Lodz before the German occupation of Poland? What was their everyday life like in the ghetto? Why are there so many photos in which Mendel Grossman shows life behind barbed wire? How did Abraham Lewin's diary describing deportations from the Warsaw ghetto come to be found? What does Gusta Davidson-Draenger, the head of a Jewish resistance group, say about imprisonment by the Gestapo? What does the memorial mean for Sabina van der Linden, née Haberman, who gave a speech at the inauguration ceremony in May 2005 and whose family biography is charted in the Room of Families? Another way for groups to creatively engage with what they have seen and experienced is to produce their own memorial design in the form of a collage or drawing. Alternatively, a walking tour of the district around the memorial shows the varied landscape of memory in Berlin.

Following the lengthy debates prior to the inauguration of the memorial, one commentator raised smiles by saying that he hoped it would be *"a place where one likes to go"*.

The remark was initially regarded as strange in relation to a place of remembrance and admonition, but the sentiment has since come to fruition. The Memorial to the Murdered Jews of Europe, commonly known as the Holocaust Memorial, has long since become a place of learning, a place where people meet and exchange opinions, and a place of respectful remembrance.

Statistical and Technical Information

Field of Stelae

Area of the Field of Stelae: 19,073 m²

Number of stelae: 2,711 (all made of concrete)

Dimensions of the stelae: width 0.95 m, length 2.38 m height between 0 and 4.7 m, inclination from 0.5° to 2°

Weight of the biggest, 4.7 m high stelae: approx. 16 t

Average weight of the stelae: approx. 8 t

Layout of the stelae: a grid pattern with 54 rows running north to south and 87 running east to west

Area of paved surfaces: approx. 13,100 m²

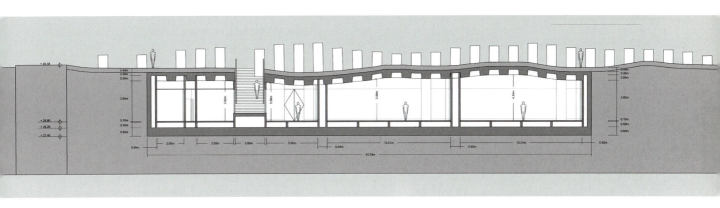

Lighting:
180 lights set into the paved surface at ground level

Total area of the Information Centre:
2,116 m², of which 778 m² is exhibition space

Time between the original proposal for the memorial and its inauguration: 17 years (1987 to 2005)

Total construction cost:
27.6 million euros (from state funds)

Visitor Numbers

Since the inauguration of the Memorial to the Murdered Jews of Europe in May 2005, millions of people have visited the Field of Stelae and by autumn 2009 over two million people had visited the exhibition in the Information Centre. There are over 450,000 visitors from all over the world to the Information Centre each year and in busy periods the Centre receives over 2,300 visitors per day.

Around 40 freelance staff are responsible for the guided tours of the Field of Stelae and visitor services at the Information Centre. The international nature of the team means that tours can currently be offered in around 20 languages. The free information leaflet is available in 14 languages. Most visitors are from German or English-speaking countries. The educational services offered by the memorial are also very popular, with over 2,300 guided visits, workshops and study days for school or adult groups being organised annually.

Minister of State Bernd Neumann greeting the millionth visitor to the Information Centre, June 12, 2007.

Aerial view of the construction site of the memorial with the "protective cover" over the Information Centre, March 2004.

Use of Technology and New Media

On account of the restricted space in the Information Centre, it was clear from the early planning stages that the exhibition would make extensive use of multimedia resources. Hence, there are six multimedia points in the Information Centre. There are four databases, three of which are interactive. The exhibition has eight data projectors, 15 interactive computer stations, four screen-based presentations and six audio points. 17 kilometres of cable were laid for the multimedia facilities alone. In addition, both seminar rooms are fully-equipped with multimedia resources. The advanced technology makes it possible to use conventional formats to play and present information via an "interface" in the wall. It is also possible to merge the two rooms into one larger space in which press conferences, book presentations and panel discussions can take place.

In view of the large number of visitors to the Information Centre, it is obviously crucial that technical resources are available, durable and user-friendly. The resources in the Information Centre reflect ongoing academic research and updates and additions to the contents of the exhibition. They are constantly being improved, developed and adapted to meet the latest technological standards.

MEMORIALS AND HISTORICAL INFORMATION IN THE AREA AROUND THE HOLOCAUST MEMORIAL

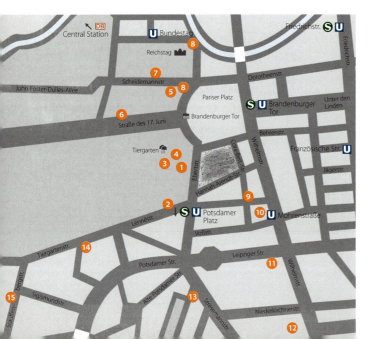

1 Memorial to the Homosexuals Persecuted under the National Socialist Regime

2 Monument to Gotthold Ephraim Lessing

3 "Global Stone" Project

4 Monument to Johann Wolfgang von Goethe

5 Memorial to the Sinti and Roma Murdered under the National Socialist Regime

6 Soviet War Memorial

7 Memorial to the Murdered Reichstag Deputies

8 "White Crosses" Memorial Site

9 Information Board "The 'Führerbunker': Myth and Historial Reality"

10 Monuments to the Prussian Military at the Former Wilhelmplatz

11 Monument to the Events of June 17, 1953

12 Topography of Terror and "Wilhelmstrasse" Historical Mile

13 Plinth of a Monument to Karl Liebknecht

14 "Operation 'T4'" Sculpture and Plaque

15 German Resistance Memorial Centre

Memorial to the Homosexuals Persecuted under the National Socialist Regime

After coming to power, the National Socialists increased the severity of the section in the Reich criminal code that outlawed homosexual acts. Homosexual men were deported to concentration camps. After 1935, an increasing number of homosexual men underwent forced castration. Lesbians were imprisoned under false accusations. Societal prejudice against homosexuals continued after 1945 and there was no talk of the injustice suffered by the victims. Germany's final provisions against homosexuality were not abolished until 1994. In 2003, the German Bundestag voted in favour of building a memorial to the homosexuals persecuted under the National Socialist regime. The memorial was inaugurated in 2008. It consists of a slightly tilted concrete stele which has a window showing a film of two men kissing. The memorial is also intended to "create a lasting sign of opposition to hostility, intolerance and the marginalisation of gay men and lesbians".

Monument to Gotthold Ephraim Lessing

In the 1850s, the idea came about to construct monuments to writers and poets as a way of encouraging pride in a single German nation among the individual German-speaking states. Established by citizens' committees, these projects were overseen by the Prussian King and, after 1871, the Kaiser (German Emperor). The history of the Lessing monument reveals the limits to the integration of German Jews at the time. A Jewish monument committee was established in 1886 with the explicit aim of honouring this writer as a champion of tolerance. Once the monument had been unveiled at the end of 1890, the conservative and Catholic press started to criticise what they considered to be the inappropriate commemoration of Lessing based on political liberalism. Those who admired Lessing for his role in the Enlightenment and as a voice of reconciliation saw themselves classed as "enemies of Christ" and "critics of all forms of authoritarian belief". Anti-Jewish sentiment was clearly voiced in the process. Such criticism diminished the impact of the monument at the time.

"Global Stone" Project

During his sailing trips around the world, Wolfgang Kraker von Schwarzenfeld encountered global problems such as war and environmental damage. As a result, he decided to establish the project "Global Stone", which is financed by sponsors. Starting in 1999, he searched in each continent for two stones weighing approximately 30 tonnes and with unique characteristics in terms of material, form or history. One of each pair of stones remains in its country of origin and the other is placed in the Tiergarten Park in Berlin. Each stone, and thereby each continent, is intended to represent five steps towards peace: Europe stands for awakening, Africa for hope, Asia for forgiveness, America for love and Australia for peace. The stones are positioned in such a way that once a year, on June 21, the light reflected from the stones forms an invisible connection between the "sister stones" in the various parts of the world and in Berlin as well as between the five Berlin stones. This connection is intended to symbolise the unity of mankind.

Monument to Johann Wolfgang von Goethe

In 1880, a monument to Johann Wolfgang von Goethe was unveiled in Berlin's Tiergarten Park in the presence of the German Emperor and the German Crown Prince. However, the construction of this monument had met with delays. After the foundation stone had been laid for a Friedrich Schiller statue on Gendarmenmarkt square in 1859, there were lengthy and heated debates about the possibility of erecting a group of monuments to Schiller, Lessing and Goethe. Ultimately, however, the Schiller monument was built without any accompanying statues. There was a muted public response to the Goethe monument. Prior to the foundation of the German Reich in 1871, the poet laureate had been seen to represent "the German desire for a nation", but some now suspected him of having had "cosmopolitan ideals". Further monuments to writers and composers were erected in the Tiergarten. In addition, Wilhelm II had the "Siegesallee" (Victory Avenue) built. This avenue, which was completed in 1901, contained 32 marble monuments of leaders, which ran in a line from Kemperplatz (now the entrance and exit of the Tiergarten underpass) to the Victory Column, which was located in front of the Reichstag at the time.

Memorial to the Sinti and Roma Murdered under the National Socialist Regime

For many years there was little public acknowledgement of the genocide of the Sinti and Roma (the "Porajmos"), who were persecuted as "gypsies" under the National Socialist regime. In 1992, the German government voted to build a national memorial to the murdered Sinti and Roma, but the construction was delayed as a result of disputes between victim associations concerning the memorial's inscription. It was finally completed in 2010. The memorial consists of a fountain with a column in the centre bearing a fresh flower. Once a day the column sinks into the water and the flower is replaced. Rather than an inscription there is a quotation from the poem "Auschwitz" by the Italian writer Rom Santino Spinelli, known as Alexian: "Sunken cheeks/dead eyes/cold lips/silence/heart torn apart/breathless/speechless/no tears." In addition, there are information boards detailing the marginalisation and mass murder of this minority group throughout Europe during the National Socialist regime of terror.

Soviet War Memorial

The Soviet War Memorial was probably the first memorial to be built in the destroyed city of Berlin at the end of the war. It is dedicated to the over 20,000 members of the Red Army who died in the battle of Berlin. The memorial grounds are also a graveyard for over 2,000 Soviet soldiers. The memorial consists of the graves, an eight metre high bronze sculpture of a soldier and two "T 34" tanks, which were the first to reach Berlin in 1945. The memorial was inaugurated on November 11, 1945. Two additional, much larger, memorials were constructed in May 1949 and November 1949 in the Treptow and Schönholzer Heide areas of Berlin. Soviet soldiers were present at the memorial in Tiergarten until 1994, even though the memorial was located in the British sector of Berlin. During the Cold War, citizens of West Berlin held demonstrations here to protest against the policies of the Soviet Union. Since the withdrawal of the former Allied power after unification, all three war memorials have been maintained by the German state.

Memorial to the Murdered Reichstag Deputies

Some of the elected members of the German Reichstag were among the first victims of National Socialist persecution. Communists and Social Democrats in particular were forced into exile or underground by the new regime or else deported to concentration camps, where they were tortured and murdered. Back in 1985, the West Berlin House of Deputies submitted a motion to the Bundestag calling for the commemoration of these victims. The proposal to place a memorial in front of the Reichstag building was realised following concerted efforts by the citizens' initiative "Perspektive Berlin". The memorial was erected in 1992. It consists of 96 cast iron plates, each dedicated to one of the murdered political representatives. The plates bear the name and place and date of death of the deputies. The memorial is designed so that it can be extended if further victims are identified during the course of research into the period. The cellar of the Reichstag building houses the "Archive of German Members of Parliament", a work by the artist Christian Boltanski, which remembers the democratically elected members of parliament from 1919 to 1999.

"White Crosses" Memorial Site

The names of 136 of those who died attempting to cross the Berlin Wall to freedom are known. The citizens of West Berlin started to place crosses at the sites of these fatal escape attempts soon after the wall was built. However, it was difficult to maintain the crosses as the numbers increased and as they were spread all over the city. For this reason, the Berlin "Citizens Association" took a selection of the crosses and put them up behind the eastern side of the Reichstag on the banks of the River Spree on August 13, 1971, the 10th anniversary of the construction of the Berlin Wall. Following the fall of the Wall and unification in 1989–90 the crosses were moved from the banks of the River Spree to the Ebertstrasse during construction work on the parliament buildings, but they were returned there in 2003. The memorial in Scheidemannstrasse (on the corner of Ebertstrasse) has remained as it was. The same names are listed at both sites. These include Chris Gueffroy, who, at the age of 20, became the last person to be shot dead by GDR border guards, just nine months before the fall of the Wall.

Information Board "The 'Führerbunker': Myth and Historical Reality"

Around 200 metres from the Holocaust Memorial in Gertrud-Kolmar-Strasse (at the corner of the street In den Ministergärten), there is an information board entitled "The 'Führerbunker': Myth and Historical Reality". This marks the site of the former bunker beneath the New Reich Chancellery, which from mid-January 1945 served as the nerve centre for a war which had already long been lost. This was where Adolf Hitler committed suicide on April 30, 1945. Soviet army engineers attempted unsuccessfully to blow up the bunker in 1947. The GDR government also tried to blow up the bunker in 1959, but it remained largely intact. The site was levelled and then forgotten about on account of its location right next to the Berlin Wall. In the late 1980s, the East Berlin authorities uncovered the bunker during the redevelopment of the Wilhelmstrasse (at the time Otto-Grotewohl-Strasse) and later built a car park where it used to be. In 2006, the association "Berliner Unterwelten" (Berlin Underworlds) put up an informative, factual information board "so as to avoid the construction of a myth surrounding the bunker".

Monuments to the Prussian Military at the Former Wilhelmplatz

The former Wilhelmplatz and the Wilhelmstrasse were built from 1721 during the expansion of "Friedrichstadt", a now central area of Berlin. Statues of four fallen Prussian generals were put up there after the end of the Seven Years War in 1763. In 1794 and 1828, two additional monuments – initially intended for different locations – were erected. These monuments were also dedicated to important members of the Prussian military: Leopold I, Prince of Anhalt-Dessau (the "Old Dessauer"), and Hans Joachim von Zieten. They were originally built in marble by Johann Gottfried Schadow, but replaced by cast bronze statues in 1859. The six statues dominated the square until the 1930s. The surrounding area, which was home to the administrative headquarters of the National Socialists, was reduced to rubble during the war and the statues were put into storage following an air raid in early 1944. Following an initiative by the Schadow Association in Berlin, the statues of Zieten and Anhalt-Dessau were returned to their historical location in 2003 and 2005 respectively, and the remaining four statues were returned in 2009.

Monument to the Events of June 17, 1953

Of all the buildings in the centre of Berlin, the current Federal Ministry of Finance symbolises the history of the last century like no other. The building became the Reich Aviation Ministry in 1935–36, housed the offices of Hermann Göring and served as one of the headquarters of the National Socialist regime. The office building was barely damaged in the war and it became the headquarters of the Soviet military administration in 1945. The founding of the GDR was announced in the banquet hall on October 7, 1949. Until 1989, various GDR government departments were located in this building, which was known as the "House of Ministries". For this reason, it was targeted by the approximately 10,000 workers protesting against conditions in the GDR on June 17, 1953. This demonstration was part of the people's uprising, which was crushed by Soviet tanks. From 1991 to 1995, the building housed the "Treuhand", the agency that privatised East German enterprises. A memorial consisting of a glass panel with photographs of the workers' protest was inaugurated at this building on June 16, 2000, ten years after German unification.

Topography of Terror and "Wilhelmstrasse" Historical Mile

The headquarters of the Gestapo and SS were located in Prinz-Albrecht-Strasse (now Niederkirchnerstrasse), on the corner of Wilhelmstrasse. This was the National Socialist headquarters responsible for the persecution of political opponents and the mass murder of European Jews and other groups. The buildings were destroyed or damaged during the war and the ruins cleared after 1945. An exhibition around the exposed foundations has been located at this historic site since 1987. In 2010, the Topography of Terror Foundation will open a permanent exhibition in a new building.

The Wilhelmstrasse had served as the headquarters of Prussian ministries since the 19th century. It later became the power centre of the Third Reich and the National Socialists. The GDR government used some of the buildings that had escaped war damage. These are now the headquarters of some of the ministries of unified Germany. The Topography of Terror's project "Wilhelmstrasse Historical Mile" (Geschichtsmeile Wilhelmstrasse), established in 1996, uses text and images to detail the history of the individual buildings.

Plinth of a Monument to Karl Liebknecht

On May 1, 1916 Karl Liebknecht, the Reichstag deputy and co-founder of the "Spartacus League", spoke at an anti-war demonstration near Potsdamer Platz. Liebknecht was arrested at the demonstration. Following his release he continued his political work and took part in the "November Revolution". On November 9, 1918 he pronounced the "Free Socialist Republic" from the balcony of the Berlin City Palace. On August 13, 1951 the foundation stone was laid for what was probably the first post-war monument in East Berlin. However, consensus could not be reached over the form of this monument to the "workers' leader" and following the construction of the Berlin Wall on August 13, 1961 the monument's plinth remained in the "no-man's land" around the border. In 1995 it was removed and placed into storage during construction work. Following an initiative by the association "Active Museum", the Berlin district of Mitte returned the monument to its original location in November 2003 as a "Record of the City's History". It is accompanied by an information board.

"Operation 'T4'" Sculpture and Plaque

The handicapped were among the first victims of the National Socialist extermination policy. In 1940–41, over 70,000 patients of German clinics and care homes were classed as "unworthy of life" and murdered in custom-built killing centres as part of the "euthanasia" operation. Public opposition led the SS to halt this programme of organised killing, but doctors in the centres continued to murder patients on their own initiative. Tiergartenstrasse 4 was the headquarters of the organisation that under the codename Operation "T4" initiated, coordinated and implemented the mass murders between 1940 and 1945. A sculpture originally intended for an exhibition in the Martin Gropius Building was put up to recall the crimes in 1987. A plaque to the victims was added in 1989. In 2008–09, a Grey Bus Memorial by the German artist Horst Hoheisel was located at the site of the former T4 headquarters. There are ongoing discussions on what to do with this historical site in the future.

German Resistance Memorial Centre

The "Bendler Block", the building housing the former High Command of the German Army, was at the centre of the plot to assassinate Hitler on July 20, 1944, led by Colonel Claus Schenk Graf von Stauffenberg. The main participants, including Stauffenberg, were shot dead in the courtyard of the building just past midnight on July 21. A monument was unveiled at the site in 1953 by Ernst Reuter, mayor of West Berlin. A plaque was put up in 1962 listing the names of the murdered officers and the commemorative courtyard was redesigned in 1980. A memorial site and educational centre were established at this historical location in 1968, and since 1989 there has been a detailed permanent exhibition charting various forms of resistance against the National Socialist regime in Europe. In 1993, the Berlin headquarters of the Federal Ministry of Defence also moved into the complex of buildings. In 2009, a monument to Bundeswehr soldiers who have been killed or lost their lives in the course of duty was opened on the site.

The following publications are available in the Information Centre and in bookshops.

The Holocaust Memorial

Ute Heimrod, Günter Schlusche, Horst Seferens (eds.): Der Denkmalstreit – das Denkmal? Die Debatte um das "Denkmal für die ermordeten Juden Europas". Eine Dokumentation. Berlin 1999.

Jan-Holger Kirsch: Nationaler Mythos oder historische Trauer? Der Streit um ein zentrales "Holocaust-Mahnmal" für die Berliner Republik. Cologne et al. 2003.

Hans-Georg Stavginski: Das Holocaust-Denkmal. Der Streit um das "Denkmal für die ermordeten Juden Europas" in Berlin (1988–1999). Paderborn et al. 2002.

Claus Leggewie, Erik Meyer: "Ein Ort, an den man gerne geht". Das Holocaust-Mahnmal und die deutsche Geschichtspolitik nach 1989. Munich, Vienna 2005.

Stiftung Denkmal für die ermordeten Juden Europas (eds.): Materialien zum Denkmal für die ermordeten Juden Europas. Berlin 2005.

Stiftung Denkmal für die ermordeten Juden Europas (eds.): Denkmal für die ermordeten Juden Europas – Fotografien von Klaus Frahm. Berlin 2005.

Location

Dietmar Arnold: Neue Reichskanzlei und "Führerbunker". Legenden und Wirklichkeit. Berlin 2005.

Laurenz Demps: Berlin-Wilhelmstraße. Eine Topographie preußisch-deutscher Macht. Berlin 2000.

Sibylle Quack: Cora Berliner, Gertrud Kolmar, Hannah Arendt – Straßen am Denkmal ehren ihr Andenken. Teetz 2005.

Stiftung Topographie des Terrors: Die Wilhelmstraße – Regierungsviertel im Wandel. Berlin 2007.

Work of the Foundation

Stiftung Denkmal für die ermordeten Juden Europas, Günter Schlusche, in Zusammenarbeit mit der Akademie der Künste (eds.): Architektur der Erinnerung – NS-Verbrechen in der europäischen Gedenkkultur. Berlin 2006.

Stiftung Denkmal für die ermordeten Juden Europas, Jürgen Lillteicher, in collaboration with Stiftung "Erinnerung, Verantwortung und Zukunft" (eds.): Profiteure des NS-Systems? Deutsche Unternehmen und das Dritte Reich. Berlin 2006.

Stiftung Denkmal für die ermordeten Juden Europas, Ulrich Baumann und Magnus Koch (Hrsg.): "Was damals Recht war …" – Soldaten und Zivilisten vor Gerichten der Wehrmacht. Berlin 2008.

Andreas Nachama, Uwe Neumärker, Hermann Simon (eds.): "Es brennt!" – Antijüdischer Terror im November 1938. Berlin 2008.

Stiftung Denkmal für die ermordeten Juden Europas, Daniel Baranowski (eds.): "Ich bin die Stimme der sechs Millionen" – Das Videoarchiv im Ort der Information. Berlin 2009.

Front cover, page 2, 7, 20, 26, 32, 38, 46, 54, 61, 62, 84, 85:
Marko Priske, Berlin
Inside flap of the front an rear cover, page 70: buschfeld.com
Page 3 left: United States Holocaust Memorial Museum,
Washington
Page 3 centre: Państwowe Muzeum Auschwitz-Birkenau,
Oświęcim
Page 3 right: Jewish Historical Museum, Amsterdam
Page 4 left and centre, 18, 22, 56: Yad Vashem, Jerusalem
Page 4 right: F.F.D.J.F., Paris
Page 8: Dirk Nazarenus
Page 10: German-Russian Museum Berlin-Karlshorst,
Timofej Melnik collection
Page 12: Berlin State Archives
Page 13: German Federal Archives Koblenz (ADN / Robert Roeske)
Page 15, 49, 51, 52, 53, 60, 63, 66, 67, 69, 71, 72, 73, 74,
76, 77, 78, 79, 80, 82, 83: Foundation Memorial to the Murdered Jews
of Europe
Page 16, 17, 35 left: Hamburg State Archives
Page 24: Federal Archives, Ludwigsburg
Page 27, 28: Sabina van der Linden-Wolanski, Sidney
Page 31: Raphael Pijade
Page 35 right: Naphtali Brezniak
Page 37: Private collection of A. Gafni
Page 40: The Emanuel Ringelblum Historical Institute, Warsaw

Page 41: Parafia Katolicka w Betżcu / Stiftung Denkmal, Berlin
Page 42: Regional Museum »dr Janusz Peter«, Tomaszów Lubelski
Page 43, 44, 45: Hamburg Institute for Social Research
Page 48: Wojciech Krynski
Page 57: Leo Baeck Institute, New York
Page 65: Plan produced by Eisenman Architects (February 2002)
showing a cross-section of the steps leading down to the
Information Centre
Page 75: Documentation and Cultural Centre of German Sinti
and Roma, Heidelberg
Page 81: Government-funded organisation devoted to the
examination and reappraisal of the Communist dictatorship
in East Germany

DKV-Edition
Memorial to the Murdered Jews of Europe
Guide to the Information Centre

Editor:
Foundation Memorial to the Murdered Jews of Europe

Responsible in the terms of the Press Law / Editorial staff:
Uwe Neumärker

Authors:
Daniel Baranowski, Ulrich Baumann, Constanze Jaiser, Adam Kerpel-Fronius, Barbara Köster, Uwe Neumärker, Uwe Seemann, Grischa Zeller

With support from Felizitas Borzym, Leonie Mechelhoff, Anja Sauter

Translation:
Caroline Pearce

Layout and Production:
Edgar Endl

The Foundation Memorial to the Murdered Jews of Europe is a federal foundation under public law, which supervises the Memorial to the Murdered Jews of Europe, the Memorial to the Homosexuals Persecuted under the National Socialist Regime and the Memorial to the Sinti and Roma Murdered under the National Socialist Regime. Moreover, its mission is to endeavour to "ensure that all victims of National Socialism are remembered and honoured appropriately", and to refer the public to "authentic memorial sites".

Further information: www.stiftung-denkmal.de

Reproduction:
Lanarepro, Lana (Südtirol)

Printing and Binding:
F&W Mediencenter, Kienberg

Bibliographic information published by the Deutsche Nationalbibliothek
The Deutsche Nationalbibliothek lists this publication in the Deutsche Nationalbibliografie; detailed bibliographic data are available in the internet at http://dnb.d-nb.de

ISBN 978-3-422-02236-2
© 2010 Deutscher Kunstverlag GmbH Berlin München